FRIENDS
FOREVER

Edited by Peggy Bresnick

FRIENDS
FOREVER

A Book of Quotations

**Andrews McMeel
Publishing**

Kansas City

ISBN: 0-8362-3559-2
Library of Congress Catalog Card Number: 97-71543

CONTENTS

INTRODUCTION

Life is nothing without friendship.
QUINTUS ENNIUS

IMAGINE LIFE without friends. Woven through the fabric of our lives, they are an ever-changing family of our own choice. Early friends, playgroup, or neighborhood kids are like the families we are born to: Friendly, hostile, or indifferent, we are thrown together.

Later companions take on a more diverse cast, shifting as we grow. If families are a glance in the mirror, friends can be a fun-house mirror. The wild friend, the thoughtful friend, the smart one, and the angry one all express parts of ourselves which branch out past the limits of our family experience, reflecting our changing selves as we explore the world.

Friends enliven work, tolerate our moods, add spice and humor to our days, brighten the dark times, and generally bring out the best in us. They come and go, mixing with each other, or not. Some are with us from cradle to grave, regardless of the years and miles between. Others pass through like a whim and are forgotten; all make their marks on us. Good friends can outlast lovers, and know us better than our families do. This collection celebrates the many faces and joys of friendship.

NEW FRIENDS

A sudden thought strikes me,
—let us swear an eternal friendship.

J. Hookham Frere

No man is the whole of himself.
His friends are the rest of him.

proverb

In my friend, I find a second self.

ISABEL NORTON

To know of someone here and there
whom we accord with, who is living on
with us, even in silence—this makes our
earthly ball a peopled garden.

Johann Wolfgang von Goethe

Wilhelm Meister's Apprenticeship

Develop the art of friendliness. One can experience a variety of emotions staying home and reading or watching television; one will be alive but hardly living. Most of the meaningful aspects of life are closely associated with people. Even the dictionary definition of life involves people.

William L. Abbott

My wife once said that she likes me to be at home, in my own study. She doesn't want to talk to me, or to see me, but she likes to think I'm there. That's exactly how I feel about the small number of my oldest friends.

Sir Walter Raleigh

A life without a friend is a life without a sun.

GERMAN PROVERB

Two may talk together under the same roof for many years, yet never really meet; and two others at first speech are old friends.

Mary Catherwood

You meet your friend, your face brightens—you have struck gold.

Kassia

Celebrate the happiness that friends
    are always giving,
make every day a holiday and celebrate
    just living!

Amanda Bradley

---

*Have friends.
'Tis a second
existence.*

BALTASAR GRACIÁN

When the sun shines on you, you see your friends. Friends are the thermometers by which one may judge the temperature of our fortunes.

Marguerite Blessington

It is good to have friends, even in hell.

When friends ask for a second cup
they are open to conversation.

Gail Parent

A friend may well be reckoned the masterpiece of nature.

Ralph Waldo Emerson

Wishing to be friends is quick work,
but friendship is a slow-ripening fruit.

Aristotle

There was a definite process by which one made people into friends, and it involved talking to them and listening to them for hours at a time.

Rebecca West

Friendship's the wine of life.

EDWARD YOUNG

Stay is a charming word in a friend's vocabulary.

Louisa May Alcott

Some of the most rewarding and beautiful moments of a friendship happen in the unforeseen open spaces between planned activities. It is important that you allow these spaces to exist.

*Christine Leefeldt
and Ernest Callenbach*

The ornament of a house is the friends who frequent it.

Ralph Waldo Emerson

Mighty proud I am that I am able to have a spare bed for my friends.

Samuel Pepys

It is the steady and merciless increase of occupations, the augmented speed at which we are always trying to live, the crowding of each day with more work than it can profitably hold, which has cost us, among other good things, the undisturbed enjoyment of friends. Friendship takes time, and we have no time to give it.

Agnes Repplier

If the first law of friendship is that it has to be cultivated, the second law is to be indulgent when the first law has been neglected.

Voltaire

We secure our friends not by accepting favors but by doing them.

Thucydides

A friend is a speaking acquaintance who also listens.

Arthur H. Glasgow

You can make more friends in two months by becoming more interested in other people than you can in two years by trying to get people interested in you.

Dale Carnegie

*The ones that
give, get back
in kind.*

PAM DURBAN

Friendship is not a fruit for enjoyment only, but also an opportunity for service.

Greek proverb

An acquaintance that begins with a compliment is sure to develop into a real friendship.

Oscar Wilde

There is nothing final between friends.

WILLIAM JENNINGS BRYAN

One loyal friend is worth ten thousand relatives.

Euripides

Friendship multiplies the good of life and divides the evil. 'Tis the sole remedy against misfortune, the very ventilation of the soul.

Baltasar Gracián

Friendship is a plant we must often water.

GERMAN PROVERB

So long as there is still a little friendship and a desire to help each other—so long as all that is real . . . that is sufficient for a man's short span of life.

Nathan Bistritzki

A sympathetic friend can be quite as dear as a brother.

Homer

The Odyssey

I love you not only for what you have made of yourself, but for what you are making of me.

Roy Croft

Friendship is a

magic weaver.

PROVERB

Think where man's glory most begins
        and ends
And say my glory was I had such friends.

William Butler Yeats

There's nothing worth the wear of
winning,
But laughter and the love of friends.

Hilaire Belloc

HONESTY IS BEST

Friends do not live in harmony merely,
as some say, but in melody.

Henry David Thoreau

I would
Prefer as friend a good man ignorant
Than one more clever who is evil too.

Euripides

I don't like to commit myself about heaven and hell—you see, I have friends in both places.

Mark Twain

Treat your friends as you do your pictures, and place them in their best light.

Jennie Jerome Churchill

One who looks for a friend without faults will have none.

Hasidic saying

My friends were poor, but honest.

WILLIAM SHAKESPEARE

All's Well That Ends Well

The happiest moments my heart knows are those in which it is pouring forth its affections to a few esteemed characters.

Thomas Jefferson

No receipt openeth the heart but a true friend, to whom you may impart griefs, joys, fears, hopes, suspicions, counsels, and whatsoever lieth upon the heart to oppress it, in a kind of civil shrift or confession.

Francis Bacon

*A joy shared is
a joy doubled.*

JOHANN WOLFGANG
VON GOETHE

*Friendship is
like two clocks
keeping time.*

ANONYMOUS

A true friend is the greatest of all blessings, and that which we take the least care of all to acquire.

La Rochefoucauld

To throw away an honest friend is, as it were, to throw your life away.

Sophocles

Oedipus the King

Unless you bear with the faults of a friend you betray your own.

Publilius Syrus

Nobody who is afraid of laughing,
and heartily too, at his friend, can be said
to have a true and thorough love for him.

*Julius Charles Hare
and Augustus William Hare*

A friend is one who knows all about you and likes you anyway.

Christi Mary Warner

It's funny how your initial approach to a person can determine your feelings toward them, no matter what facts develop later on.

Dorothy Uhnak

You can always tell a real friend: When you've made a fool of yourself he doesn't feel you've done a permanent job.

Laurence J. Peter

Why do people lament their follies for which their friends adore them?

Gerard Hopkins

Writers seldom choose as friends those self-contained characters who are never in trouble, never unhappy or ill, never make mistakes, and always count their change when it is handed to them.

Catherine Drinker Bowen

True friendship is never serene.

MARIE DE SÉVIGNÉ

Every man should have a fair-sized cemetery in which to bury the faults of his friends.

Henry Brooks Adams

A friend should be a master at guessing and keeping still.

Friedrich Nietzsche

I always felt that the great high privilege, relief, and comfort of friendship was that one had to explain nothing.

Katherine Mansfield

A friend is a person with whom I may be sincere. Before him, I may think aloud.

Ralph Waldo Emerson

Friendship closes its eyes rather than see the moon eclipst; while malice denies that it is ever at the full.

Julius Charles Hare
and Augustus William Hare

Have patience with a friend rather than lose him forever.

Arab proverb

If we would build on a sure foundation in friendship, we must love friends for their sake rather than for our own.

Charlotte Brontë

A friend who loved perfection would be a perfect friend, did not that love shut his door on me.

Logan Smith

Between friends, frequent reproofs make the friendship distant.

Confucius

The proper office of a friend is to side with you when you are in the wrong. Nearly anybody will side with you when you are in the right.

Mark Twain

Sooner or later you've heard all your best friends have to say. Then comes the tolerance of real love.

Ned Rorem

The essence of true friendship is
to make allowance for another's little
lapses.

David Storey

Friendships, like marriages, are dependent on avoiding the unforgivable.

John D. MacDonald

Without reciprocal mildness and temperance there can be no continuance of friendship. Every man will have something to do for his friend, and something to bear with in him.

Owen Felltham

It is more shameful to distrust one's friends than to be deceived by them.

La Rochefoucauld

A friend should bear his friend's infirmities.

WILLIAM SHAKESPEARE

Julius Caesar

When my friends are one-eyed, I look at them in profile.

Joseph Joubert

Do not use a hatchet to remove a fly from your friend's forehead.

Chinese proverb

It is well, when one is judging a friend, to remember that he is judging you with the same godlike and superior impartiality.

Arnold Bennett

Never speak ill of yourself. Your friends will always say enough on that subject.

Charles Maurice de Talleyrand

If all persons knew what they said of each other there would not be four friends in the world.

Blaise Pascal

What I cannot love, I overlook.
Is that real friendship?

Anaïs Nin

Instead of loving your enemies, treat your friends a little better.

Edgar Howe

To find a friend one must close one eye—to keep him, two.

Norman Douglas

Friends will be much apart. They will respect more each other's privacy than their communion.

Henry David Thoreau

If we were all given by magic the power to read each other's thoughts, I suppose the first effect would be to dissolve all friendships.

Bertrand Russell

We know our friends by their defects rather than by their merits.

W. Somerset Maugham

Friendship may sometimes step a few paces in advance of truth; and who would check her?

Walter Savage Landor

If we all said to people's faces what we say behind one another's backs, society would be impossible.

Honoré de Balzac

When someone tells you the truth, lets you think for yourself, experience your own emotions, he is treating you as a true equal. As a friend.

Whitney Otto

Friendship either finds or makes equals.

PUBLILIUS SYRUS

There can be no friendship where there is no freedom. Friendship loves a free air, and will not be fenced up in straight and narrow enclosures.

William Penn

Between friends there is no need of justice.

ARISTOTLE

You cannot be friends upon any other terms than upon the terms of equality.

Woodrow Wilson

The more we love our friends, the less we flatter them; it is by excusing nothing that pure love shows itself.

Jean Baptiste Molière

Le Misanthrope

Have no friends not equal to your-self.

CONFUCIUS

Never have a companion who casts
you in the shade.

Baltasar Gracián

No person is your friend who demands your silence, or denies your right to grow.

Alice Walker

In friendship we find nothing false or insincere; everything is straightforward, and springs from the heart.

Cicero

Rather the bite of a friend than the kiss of an enemy.

Shalom Aleichem

"The Adventures of Menachem Mendl"

I can trust my friends. . . . These people force me to examine myself, encourage me to grow.

Cher

Better a nettle in the side of your friend than his echo.

Ralph Waldo Emerson

A companion loves some agreeable
qualities which a man may possess, but a
friend loves the man himself.

James Boswell

*A good friend
is my nearest
relation.*

THOMAS FULLER, M.D.

Friendship is a strong and habitual inclination in two persons to promote the good and happiness of one another.

Eustace Budgell

The friendships which last are those wherein each friend respects the other's dignity to the point of not really wanting anything from him.

Cyril Connolly

The condition which high friendship
demands is ability to do without it.

Ralph Waldo Emerson

The heart may think it knows better:
The senses know that absence blots
people out. We have really no absent
friends.

Elizabeth Bowen

Odd how much it hurts when a friend moves away—and leaves behind only silence.

Pam Brown

On the road between the homes of friends, grass does not grow.

Norwegian proverb

A friend can tell you things you don't want to tell yourself.

Frances Ward Weller

Wherever you are it is your own
friends who make your world.

William James

TRUE
FRIENDSHIP

Every man passes his life in the search after friendship.

Ralph Waldo Emerson

Sometimes, with luck, we find the kind of true friend, male or female, that appears only two or three times in a lucky lifetime, one that will winter us and summer us, grieve, rejoice, and travel with us.

Barbara Holland

*A friend is a
gift you give
yourself.*

ROBERT LOUIS STEVENSON

If I don't have friends, then I ain't got nothin'.

Billie Holiday

The loneliest woman in the world is a woman without a close woman friend.

Toni Morrison

Friendship is a creature formed for a
companionship, not for a herd.

Michel de Montaigne

A friend is worth all hazards we can run.

EDWARD YOUNG

One's friends are that part of the human race with which one can be human.

George Santayana

A good friend—like a tube of toothpaste—comes through in a tight squeeze.

Anonymous

In time of prosperity friends will be plenty; in time of adversity not one in twenty.

English proverb

We have fewer friends than we imagine, but more than we know.

Hugo von Hofmannsthal

A true friend will see you through
when others see that you are through.

Laurence J. Peter

The test of friendship is assistance in adversity—and that, too, unconditional assistance. . . . Conditional cooperation is like adulterated cement which does not bind.

Mohandas K. Gandhi

He who has a thousand friends
has not a friend to spare.
And he who has one enemy will
meet him everywhere.

Ali

The shifts of fortune test the reliability of friends.

Cicero

You will always have the countenance of friends whilst fortune favors you.

Ovid

A true friend is one who likes you despite your achievements.

Arnold Bennett

It is in the character of very few men to honor without envy a friend who has prospered.

Aeschylus

Give me one friend, just one,
  who meets
The needs of all my varying moods.

Esther M. Clark

I had only one friend, my dog. My wife was mad at me, and I told her a man ought to have at least two friends. She agreed—and bought me another dog.

Pepper Rodgers

Show me a friend who will weep with me; those who will laugh with me I can find myself.

Yugoslav proverb

He gave to Mis'ry all he had, a tear;
He gain'd from Heav'n ('twas all he
wish'd) a friend.

Thomas Gray

Love is rarer than genius itself. And
friendship is rarer than love.

Charles Pequy

The easiest kind of relationship for me is with ten thousand people. The hardest is with one.

Joan Baez

Nine-tenths of the people were created so you would want to be with the other tenth.

Horace Walpole

Friendship with the wise gets better with time, as a good book gets better with age.

Thiruvalluvar

Friendship is the hobbyhorse of all the moral rhetoricians; it is nectar and ambrosia to them.

Immanuel Kant

A friend's only gift is himself. . . .
We are not to look now for what makes
friendships useful, but for whatever may
be found in friendship that may lend
utility to life.

George Santayana

*Friendship is
a furrow in the
sand.*

Tongan proverb

In prosperity our friends know us; in adversity we know our friends.

Churton Collins

Those who have suffered understand
suffering and therefore extend their hand.

Patti Smith

Friendship is the allay of our sorrows,
the ease of our passions, the discharge
of our oppressions, the sanctuary to our
calamities, the counsellor of our doubts,
the clarity of our minds, the emission of
our thoughts, the exercise and improve-
ment of what we meditate.

Jeremy Taylor

However rare true love may be, it is less so than true friendship.

La Rochefoucauld

True friendship is like sound health;
the value of it is seldom known until it
be lost.

Charles Caleb Colton

How often we find ourselves turning our backs on our actual friends, that we may go and meet their ideal cousins.

Henry David Thoreau

Really, one has some friends, and when one comes to think about it, it is impossible to tell how one ever became friendly with them.

Françoise Mallet-Joris

The real friendships among men are so
rare that when they occur they are famous.

Clarence Day

Friendship is a word, the very sight of which in print makes the heart warm.

Augustine Birrell

Friendship's a noble name, 'tis love refined.

SUSANNAH CENTLIVRE

I loathe a friend whose gratitude
          grows old,
a friend who takes his friend's prosperity
but will not voyage with him in his grief.

Euripides

That man travels the longest journey that undertakes it in search of a sincere friend.

Ali Ibn-Abi-Talib

One friend in a lifetime is much;
two are many; three are hardly possible.

Henry Adams

True friendship is a plant of slow growth and must undergo and withstand the shocks of adversity before it is entitled to the appellation.

George Washington

Hold a true friend with both your hands.

NIGERIAN PROVERB

My best friend is the man who in wishing me well wishes it for my sake.

Aristotle

Value friendship for what there is in it,
not for what can be gotten out of it.

H. Clay Trumbull

We do not so much need the help of our friends as the confidence of their help in need.

Epicurus

WITH FRIENDS
LIKE THESE

Against a foe I can myself defend,—
But Heaven protect me from a blundering
friend!

D'Arcy W. Thompson

God save me from my friends—I can protect myself from my enemies.

proverb

The man that hails you Tom or Jack,
And proves by thumps upon your back
How he esteems your merit,
Is such a friend, that one had need
Be very much his friend indeed
To pardon or to bear it.

William Cowper

No friend's a friend till he shall prove
a friend.

Beaumont and Fletcher

The Faithful Friends

I have no trouble with my enemies. But my goddam friends, . . . they are the ones that keep me walking the floor nights.

Warren G. Harding

There is no man so friendless but what he can find a friend sincere enough to tell him disagreeable truths.

Edward Bulwer-Lytton

To have a great man for an intimate friend seems pleasant to those who have never experienced it; those who have, fear it.

Horace

The truth that is suppressed by friends
is the readiest weapon of the enemy.

Robert Louis Stevenson

There is flattery in friendship.

WILLIAM SHAKESPEARE

Henry V

One who is our friend is fond of us:
One who is fond of us isn't necessarily
our friend.

Seneca

Thy friendship oft has made my heart
    to ache:
Do be my enemy—for friendship's sake.

William Blake

There are three friendships which are advantageous, and three which are injurious. Friendship with the upright; friendship with the sincere; and friendship with the man of much observation; these are advantages. Friendship with the man of specious airs; friendship with the insinuatingly soft; and friendship with the glib-tongued; these are injurious.

Confucius

Good friends, good books, and a
sleepy conscience: this is the ideal life.

Mark Twain

He's the kind of man who picks his friends—to pieces.

Mae West

CLOSE FRIENDS

Life is nothing without friendship.

QUINTUS ENNIUS

It is characteristic of spontaneous friendships to take on first, without inquiry and
almost at first sight, the unseen doings
and unspoken sentiments of our friends;
the parts known give us evidence enough
that the unknown parts cannot be much
amiss.

George Santayana

For what do my friends stand? Not for the clever things they say: I do not remember them half an hour after they are spoken. It is the unspoken, the unconscious, which is their reality to me.

Mark Rutherford

Each friend represents a world in us, a world possibly not born until they arrive, and it is only by this meeting that a new world is born.

Anaïs Nin

It is one of the blessings of old friends that you can afford to be stupid with them.

Ralph Waldo Emerson

Yes'm, old friends is always best, 'less you can catch a new one that's fit to make an old one out of.

Sarah Orne Jewett

The Country of the Pointed Firs

My best friend is the one who brings
out the best in me.

Henry Ford

One cannot help using his early friends as the seaman uses the log, to mark his progress.

Oliver Wendell Holmes Sr.

A man has confidence in untried friends, he remembers the many offers of service so freely made by boon companions when he wanted them not; he has hope—the hope of happy inexperience.

Charles Dickens

No soul is desolate as long as there is a human being for whom it can feel trust and reverence.

George Eliot

Friendship that flames goes out in a flash.

THOMAS FULLER, M.D.

People's lives change. To keep all your old friends is like keeping all your old clothes—pretty soon your closet is so jammed and everything so crushed you can't find anything to wear. Help these friends when they need you; bless the years and happy times when you meant a lot to each other, but try not to have the guilts if new people mean more to you now.

Helen Gurley Brown

The friendship that can come to an end never really began.

Publilius Syrus

We can never replace a friend. When a man is fortunate enough to have several, he finds they are all different. No one has a double in friendship.

Friedrich von Schiller

If a man does not make new acquaintance as he advances through life, he will soon find himself left alone. A man, sir, should keep his friendship in constant repair.

Samuel Johnson

Sudden friendship, sure repentance.

JOHN RAY

She didn't know how to be friends with more than one person at a time.

Mary Calhoun

Julie's Tree

I find friendship to be like wine, raw
when new, ripened with age, the true old
man's milk and restorative cordial.

Thomas Jefferson

Familiarity breeds content.

ANNA QUINDLEN

A new friend is like a frozen stream in spring.

Russian proverb

Friends and flowers are charming when they are fresh.

Madame de Sartory

To attract good fortune, spend a new penny on an old friend, share an old pleasure with a new friend, and lift up the heart of a true friend by writing his name on the wings of a dragon.

Chinese proverb

There is a magic in the memory of a schoolboy friendship; it softens the heart, and even affects the nervous system of those who have no heart.

Benjamin Disraeli

Even where the affections are not strongly moved by any superior excellence, the companions of our childhood always possess a certain power over our minds which hardly any later friend can obtain.

Mary Wollstonecraft Shelley

Frankenstein

We die as often as we lose a friend.

PUBLILIUS SYRUS

To me, fair friend, you never can be old,
For as you were when first your eye I eyed,
Such seems your beauty still.

William Shakespeare

Flowers of true friendship never fade.

PROVERB

The best mirror is an old friend.

GEORGE HERBERT

A new friend is new wine;
When it grows old, you will enjoy
drinking it.

Ben Sira

Old friends are best. King James used to call for his old shoes; they were easiest for his feet.

John Selden

There are three faithful friends—an old wife, an old dog, and ready money.

Benjamin Franklin

Forsake not an old friend, for a new one
does not compare with him.

Ecclesiastes 9:10

A faithful friend is a strong protection;
A man who has found one has found a
treasure.
A faithful friend is beyond price,
And his value cannot be weighed.

Ben Sira

I am a big believer that you have to nourish any relationship. I am still very much a part of my friends' lives and they are very much a part of my life. A First Lady who does not have this source of strength and comfort can lose perspective and become isolated.

Nancy Reagan

The virtue is no less to conserve friend-ship gotten, than the wisdom was great to get and win the same.

William Painter

This communicating of a man's self to his friend works two contrary effects; for it redoubleth joys, and cutteth griefs in half.

Francis Bacon

*Birds of a
feather will
gather together.*

ROBERT BURTON

I am not of that feather to shake off
My friend when he most need me.

William Shakespeare

Timon of Athens

True friends visit us in prosperity only when invited, but in adversity they come without invitation.

Theophrastus

Friendship, of itself a holy tie,
Is made more sacred by adversity.

John Dryden

The Hind and the Panther

A man cannot be said to succeed in this life who does not satisfy one friend.

Henry David Thoreau

If I had to choose between betraying my *country* and betraying my *friend*, I hope I should have the guts to betray my *country*.

E. M. Forster

He makes no friend who never made a foe.

ALFRED, LORD TENNYSON

Greater love hath no man than this,
that a man lay down his life for his
friends.

John 15:13

When a friend

asks there is no

tomorrow.

GEORGE HERBERT

If I do vow a friendship, I'll perform it
To the last article.

William Shakespeare

Othello

A broken friendship may be solder'd,
but will never be sound.

Thomas Fuller

Friends show their love
in times of trouble, not in happiness.

Euripides

No people feel closer or more friendly than those who are on the same diet.

Anonymous

It is the friends that you can call at 4 A.M. that matter.

Marlene Dietrich

A friend is in prosperitie a pleasure, a solace in adversitie, in grief a comfort, in joy a merry companion, at all times an other I.

John Lyly

Old friends, we say, are best, when some sudden disillusionment shakes our faith in a new comrade.

Gelett Burgess

The firmest friendships have been formed in mutual adversity, as iron is most strongly united by the fiercest flame.

Charles Caleb Colton

Should auld acquaintance be forgot,
And never brought to mind?
Should auld acquaintance be forgot,
And days o' auld lang syne?

Robert Burns

Ah, how good it feels!
The hand of an old friend.

Henry Wadsworth Longfellow

FRIENDLY ADVICE

True happiness
Consists not in the multitude of friends,
But in the worth and choice.

Ben Jonson

The most I can do for my friend is simply to be his friend.

Henry David Thoreau

The essence of friendship is not getting, but sharing.

proverb

Convey thy love to thy friend as an arrow to the mark, to stick there, not as a ball against the wall, to rebound back to thee.

Francis Quarles

Life is partly what we make it, and partly what it is made by the friends whom we choose.

Tehyi Hsieh

Friendships are glued together with little kindnesses.

Mercia Tweedale

Reinforce the stitch that ties us, and I will do the same for you.

Doris Schwerin

I keep my friends as misers do their treasure, because, of all the things granted us by wisdom, none is greater or better than friendship.

Pietro Aretino

A faithful friend is a strong defense;
And he that hath found him hath found a
treasure.

Louisa May Alcott

You can keep your friends by not giving them away.

Mary Pettibone Poole

Make all good men your well-wishers
   and then, in the years' steady sifting,
Some of them turn into friends. Friends
   are the sunshine of life.

John Hay

Good friends are good for your health.

IRWIN SARASON

A friend in the court is better than a
penny in purse.

William Shakespeare

Henry IV

Acquaintance I would have,
    but when't depends
Not on the number, but the choice
    of friends.

Abraham Cowley

Love thy neighbor as thyself, but choose your neighborhood.

Louise Beal

The richer your friends, the more they will cost you.

ELIZABETH MARBURY

Friendship is not possible between two women one of whom is very well dressed.

Laurie Colwin

There is an old-time toast which is golden for its beauty. "When you ascend the hill of prosperity may you not meet a friend."

Mark Twain

The happiest business in all the world is
    that of making friends;
And no investment on the street pays
    larger dividends,
For life is more than stocks and bonds,
    and love than rate percent,
And he who gives in friendship's name
    shall reap what he has spent.

Anne S. Eaton

Business, you know, may bring money, but friendship hardly ever does.

Jane Austin

Emma

Your wealth is where your friends are.

LATIN PROVERB

*A good man
finds all the
world friendly.*

HINDUSTAN PROVERB

Give truth, and your gift will be paid
    in kind,
And honor will honor meet;
And the smile which is sweet will surely
    find
A smile that is just as sweet.

Madeline S. Bridges

It takes two to make a quarrel, but only one to end it.

Spanish proverb

Wear a smile and have friends; wear a scowl and have wrinkles.

George Eliot

Reprove your friends in secret, praise them openly.

Publilius Syrus

Though friendship is not quick to burn,
It is explosive stuff.

May Sarton

Neither make thy friend equal to a brother; but if thou shalt have made him so, be not the first to do him wrong.

Hesiod

You can hardly make a friend in a year,
but you can easily offend one in an hour.

Chinese proverb

It is wise to apply the oil of refined politeness to the mechanism of friendship.

Colette

You can win more friends with your ears than your mouth.

Anonymous

The costliness of keeping friends does not lie in what one does for them, but in what one, out of consideration for them, refrains from doing.

Henrik Ibsen

Friendship cannot live with ceremony,
nor without civility.

Lord Halifax

Friendship will not stand the strain of very much good advice for very long.

Robert Lynd

A hedge

between keeps

friendship green.

ENGLISH PROVERB

A man must eat a peck of salt with his friend before he knows him.

Miquel de Cervantes

Don Quixote

Friendship is honey—but don't eat it all.

MOROCCAN PROVERB

Friendship is not to be bought at a fair.

THOMAS FULLER

Friendship, n. A ship big enough to carry two in fair weather, but only one in foul.

Ambrose Bierce

The Devil's Dictionary

Where obligations begin, friendship ends.

ANONYMOUS

The strongest friendship yields to pride,
Unless the odds be on our side.

Jonathan Swift

Friendship is like money, easier made than kept.

SAMUEL BUTLER

The holy passion of Friendship is of so sweet and steady and loyal and enduring a nature that it will last through a whole lifetime, if not asked to lend money.

Mark Twain

Before borrowing money from a friend
decide which you need most.

American proverb

The touchstone of false friends is the day of need: By way of proof, ask a loan from your friends.

Sa'ib of Tabriz

*Don't put
your friend in
your pocket.*

IRISH PROVERB

I pretind ivry man is honest, and I believe none iv them ar-re. In that way I keep me friends an' save me money.

Finley Peter Dunne

With most people there will be no harm in occasionally mixing a grain of disdain with your treatment of them; that will make them value your friendship all the more.

Arthur Schopenhauer

Amid all the easily loved darlings of Charlie Brown's circle, obstreperous Lucy holds a special place in my heart. She fusses and fumes and she carps and complains. That's because Lucy cares. And it's the caring that counts. When we, as youngsters, would accuse our mother of picking on us her wise reply was, "All you'll get from strangers is surface pleasantry or indifference. Only someone who loves you will criticize you."

Judith Crist

We do not regret the loss of our friends by reasons of their merit, but because of our needs and for the good opinion that we believed them to have held of us.

La Rochefoucauld

Friendship is Love without his wings!

LORD BYRON

I have lost friends, some by death . . . others through sheer inability to cross the street.

Virginia Woolf

The only way
to have a friend
is to be one.

RALPH WALDO EMERSON

Love and Friendship

Oh, the comfort, the inexpressible comfort of feeling safe with a person, having neither to weigh thoughts nor measure words, but pouring them all right out, just as they are, chaff and grain together; certain that a faithful hand will take and sift them, keep what is worth keeping, and then with the breath of kindness throw the rest away.

Dinah Maria Mulock Craik

The person who tries to live alone will not succeed as a human being. His heart withers if it does not answer another heart. His mind shrinks away if he hears only the echoes of his own thoughts and finds no other inspiration.

Pearl S. Buck

When they are alone they want to be with others, and when they are with others they want to be alone. After all, human beings are like that.

Gertrude Stein

We all live on bases of shiftings sands [and] need trust.

Erma J. Fisk

Life is to be fortified by many friendships. To love, and to be loved, is the greatest happiness of existence.

Sydney Smith

Friendships multiply joys, and divide griefs.

H. G. BOHN

We cherish our friends not for their ability to amuse us, but for ours to amuse them.

Evelyn Waugh

It seems to me that trying to live without friends is like milking a bear to get cream for your morning coffee. It is a whole lot of trouble, and then not worth much after you get it.

Zora Neale Hurston

Only solitary men know the full joys of friendship. Others have their family; but to a solitary and an exile his friends are everything.

Willa Cather

Shadows on the Rock

And all people live, not by reason of any care they have for themselves, but by the love for them that is in other people.

Leo Tolstoy

Their belief in

one another seeks

no results.

DAVID MICHAELIS

The Best of Friends

Friendship is a sheltering tree.

SAMUEL TAYLOR COLERIDGE

I feel what I can only call a molecular lushness close to my face: the deep powder of friendship.

Gretel Ehrlich

Friends are God's apology for relations.

HUGH KINGSMILL

God gives us our relatives; thank God
we can choose our friends!

Ethel Watts Mumford

O friendship! Of all things the most rare, and therefore most rare because most excellent, whose comfort in misery is always sweet, and whose counsels in prosperity are ever fortunate.

John Lyly

If a man should importune me to give a reason why I loved him, I find it could no otherwise be expressed, than by making answer: because it was he, because it was I.

Michel de Montaigne

If friendship is firmly established
between two hearts, they do not need
the interchange of news.

Sa'ib of Tabriz

True friendship comes when silence
between two people is comfortable.

David Tyson Gentry

Friendship can exist only where men harmonize in their views of things human and divine.

Cicero

Friendship needs a certain parallelism
of life, a community of thought, a rivalry
of aim.

Henry Adams

The capacity for friendship usually goes with highly developed civilizations. The ability to cultivate people differs by culture and class; but on the whole, educated people have more ways to make friends. . . . In England, for instance, you find everyone in your class has read the same books. Here, people grope for something in common—like a newly engaged girl who came to me and said, "It's absolutely wonderful! His uncle and my cousin were on the same football team."

Margaret Mead

Two friendships in two breasts requires
The same aversions and desires.

Jonathan Swift

Friends are generally of the same sex, for when men and women agree, it is only in the conclusions; their reasons are always different.

George Santayana

To like and dislike the same things, this is what makes a solid friendship.

Sallust

*True friendship
is self-love at
second hand.*

WILLIAM HAZLITT

Friendship with oneself is all-important,
because without it one cannot be friends
with anyone else in the world.

Eleanor Roosevelt

I desire so to conduct the affairs of this administration that if at the end, when I come to lay down the reins of power, I have lost every other friend on earth, I shall at least have one friend left, and that friend shall be down inside of me.

Abraham Lincoln

The Soul selects her own Society—
Then—shuts the Door—

Emily Dickinson

The perfect friendship is that between good men, alike in their virtue.

Aristotle

A friend is, as it were, a second self.

CICERO

There is nothing that is meritorious but virtue and friendship; and, indeed, friendship itself is only a part of virtue.

Alexander Pope

That friendship may be at once fond and lasting, there must not only be equal virtue on each part, but virtue of the same kind; not only the same end must be proposed, but the same means must be approved by both.

Samuel Johnson

The friendships of the world are oft
Confederacies in vice, or leagues of
pleasure.

Joseph Addison

In politics . . . shared hatreds are almost always the basis of friendships.

Alexis de Tocqueville

There is no stronger bond of friendship than a mutual enemy.

Frankfort Moore

Show me your friends and I'll show you your ends.

Portuguese proverb

Most friendships are formed by caprice or by chance—mere confederacies in vice or leagues in folly.

Samuel Johnson

Tell me thy company and I will tell thee what thou art.

Miguel de Cervantes

That's what friendship means: sharing the prejudice of experience.

Charles Bukowski

Friendship is almost always the union
of a part of one mind with a part of
another; people are friends in spots.

George Santayana

I do not believe that friends are necessarily the people you like best, they are merely the people who got there first.

Peter Ustinov

What a delight it is to make friends
with someone you have despised!

Colette

Fate makes our relatives, choice makes our friends.

JACQUES DELILLE

Let him have the key of thy heart, who hath the lock of his own.

Sir Thomas Browne

In choosing a friend, go up a step.

JEWISH PROVERB

The more I traveled the more I realized that fear makes strangers of people who should be friends.

Shirley MacLaine

Friendship admits of difference of character, as love does that of sex.

Joseph Roux

What lasting joys the man attend
Who has a polished female friend.

Cornelius Whurr

Discussing the characters and foibles
of common friends is a great sweetener
and cement of friendship.

William Hazlitt

Women can form a friendship with a man very well; but to preserve it—to that end a slight physical antipathy must probably help.

Friedrich Nietzsche

No friendship is so cordial or so delicious as that of girl for girl, no hatred so intense and immovable as that of woman for woman.

W. S. Landor

Friendship among women is only a suspension of hostilities.

Comte de Rivarol

Men seem to kick friendship around like a football, but it doesn't seem to crack. Women treat it as glass and it goes to pieces.

Anne Morrow Lindbergh

Women, like princes, find few real friends.

LORD LYTTELTON

Great friendship
is never without
anxiety.

MARIE DE SÉVIGNÉ

Intimacies between women often go backwards, beginning in revelations and ending up in small talk without loss of esteem.

Elizabeth Bowen

Friendship, peculiar boon of Heav'n,
The noble mind's delight and pride,
To man and angels only giv'n,
To all the lower world denied.

Samuel Johnson

Animals are such agreeable friends,
they ask no questions, they pass no
criticisms.

George Eliot

To me, the sea is like a person—like a child that I've known a long time. It sounds crazy, I know, but when I swim in the sea I talk to it. I never feel alone when I'm out there.

Gertrude Ederle

The bird a nest,
the spider a web,
man friendship.

WILLIAM BLAKE

Friendship makes prosperity more brilliant, and lightens adversity by dividing and sharing it.

Cicero

I like a friend the better for having faults
that one can talk about.

William Hazlitt

To have a friend
be one.

VISCOUNT SAMUEL HERBERT

Friendship is constant in all other things
Save in the office and affairs of love:
Therefore all hearts in love use their own
       tongues;
Let every eye negotiate for itself
And trust no agent.

William Shakespeare

Much Ado About Nothing

A principal fruit of friendship is the ease and discharge of the fullness and swellings of the heart which passions of all kinds do cause and induce.

Francis Bacon

Friendship is the finest balm for the pangs of despised love.

Jane Austen

When adversities flow, then love ebbs; but friendship standeth stiffly in storms.

John Lyly

*Friendship is
far more delicate
than love.*

HESTER LYNCH PIOZZI

Friendship always benefits; love sometimes injures.

Seneca

A faithful friend is the medicine of life.

ECCLESIASTES 6:16

Friendship is the bond of reason.

R. B. SHERIDAN

Friendship is a disinterested commerce between equals.

Oliver Goldsmith

There is an important difference between love and friendship. While the former delights in extremes and opposites, the latter demands equality.

Françoise D'Aubegne Maintenon

In friendship, as in love, we are often more happy from the things we are ignorant of than from those we are acquainted with.

La Rochefoucauld

A woman's friendship borders more closely on love than man's. Men affect each other in the reflection of noble or friendly acts; whilst women ask fewer proofs and more signs and expressions of attachment.

Samuel Taylor Coleridge

Friendship, compounded of esteem and love, derives from one its tenderness and its permanence from the other.

Samuel Johnson

This book was typeset in Centaur, Stuyvesant, and ArenaCaps by Nina Gaskin.

Book design by Judith Stagnitto Abbate